Democracy Without Politicians

Peter Hayward

Published by Peter Hayward, 2022.

DEMOCRACY WITHOUT POLITICIANS

First edition. January 25, 2022.

Copyright © 2022 Peter Hayward.

ISBN: 979-8201004651

Written by Peter Hayward.

Table of Contents

Preface 1

The Trouble With Democracy 3

The Party System 5

Campaign Financing 9

A Brief Suggestion 11

Involved Institutions 13

A New Model 14

Choosing the Issues 21

Characteristics of the Jury 23

A Hierarchy of Juries 27

A Multi-level Jury System 28

The Preliminary Jury 30

The Main Jury 32

The Final Jury 34

Jury Groups 35

Parameters of the Jury 36

Experts 40

Bureaucracy 44

An Example of Bureaucratic Corruption 48

Corporations 53

The Media 55

Consultants 63

Classified Military and State Secrets 65

Scientific Policy 67

Industrial Policy 69

The Educational System 71

On the Covid-19 Pandemic 73

Preface

A brief (very brief) version of this book was self-published in April of 2020. One would not even call it a book, more an extended outline. I wanted at least some record of this idea to exist somewhere in case the virus got me which in the early months of 2020 before the demographics of the viruses victims was clear was weighing on my mind as it was on most people in the world. I threw the first version together in about two weeks and published it on several platforms in e-book form under the title Juristical Democracy. The idea of juristical democracy was not inspired by the pandemic however. I can remember it bouncing around inside by brain back when I lived in Vancouver, Canada which I left in the winter of 2008 to move to the province of Nova Scotia. The idea kept popping back into my head over the ensuing years which I took as a sign that it required more attention than I was giving it. Although as an incurable bookworm I had read thousands of books over the decades I had never tried to write one. I knew that writing an actual book was an ordeal for most people and that most books presented to publishers are rejected and most that are published are read by only a few thousand, or a few hundred people, but the more I played with this idea the more potential I saw in it to answer some of the deep flaws in our system of government. The response to the pandemic over the last two years revealed, to me at least, that our democracy was far more broken than I had imagined and was failing in a broad-based and fundamental way. As to why it took me two years to come out with a second version which while longer than the first version, is still very short. Well, for one thing, as I have discovered, writers block is real and is not helped by a series of events including quitting my job, moving twice, having difficulty finding a new job and generally dealing with the surreal chaos of life during the pandemic. I was also my plan from the beginning to keep this book small. So many books that I read could have been far shorter, often being mostly filler in order to justify the price and to give it an illusion of substance that is often not there. I have included only a couple of illustrative examples and no political theory or philosophy. This book was not written for a specialized audience but for ordinary people which is fitting as juristical democracy is a form of democracy designed to empower ordinary people. The book deals with the practical nuts and bolts of a jury based democratic order and how this bypasses the elitism that now weighs too heavily on our representative system. I think of juristical democracy as populism without demagoguery. I believe it represents the spirit of democracy better than any other form. Power to the people. And unlike so many others who have mouthed that phrase, I actually mean it.

Introduction

The Trouble With Democracy

At this point in the history of the West it is becoming increasingly obvious that democracy has become a bit of a sham, and perhaps more than a bit. It's main justification for existing, that government reflects the will of the majority of the people, is not borne out in reality, for as poll after poll and survey after survey show, there is an often great gulf between what the majority of the people want and what the people are in fact getting. After over two hundred years of practice too many interested parties have become far too skilled at bypassing the will of the majority and imposing their own vision on an often disagreeable populace who feel powerless to stop this process even when it is obvious to them. The present political landscape is a clown-car kabuki show of bad actors, con-artists and a conflicting mass of interest groups trying to bribe or intimidate politicians into doing their bidding. Our representatives cannot be trusted to do what they say and our present party-based system of representative democracy selects for the manipulative, the greedy and the power hungry.

The actual history of democracy is not an encouraging one. Since the ancient Greeks invented the concept 2600 years ago it has only been operative for about 250 of those years. The west has mostly been undemocratic with monarchy, oligarchy and other forms of autocracy ruling the day. The 20th century has seen the closest to the democratic ideal with the franchise extended first to women and then blacks in the west until today it is as universal as one can make it whilst maintaining an allegiance to the enlightenment rights-based regime that has been installed in the western world. But.....but.....many of the original criticisms, going all the way back to the Greeks, seem to be manifesting themselves. The majority want benefits but does not want to pay the requisite taxes to sustain those benefits and enough politicians seem willing to indulge them in the delusion that this is sustainable, at least while the politician is still in office. When those receiving benefits outvote the ones providing benefits for too long the downward spiral begins into eventual economic collapse.

The Party System

Observe the modern party system, specifically the American two-party system, which through the universal human trait of conformation bias almost forces voters into a polarized hostility. It forces a simple binary on the populace which all too easily devolves into a primal, tribalistic us/them mentality and even, especially among the more reflexively moralistic members of the culture, a good/evil binary that is becoming deeply concerning to any reasonable observer of the present scene. At present in the U.S. the inter-party conflict has taken on a darkly existential tone as if the only way the country can be saved is if the opposite party can be destroyed. In the recent elections, both in 2016 and 2020, it appears that half the population thinks that the opposing party has either stolen the election outright or somehow been victim of electoral malfeasance by Russia or China or Facebook or all of the above. Social media corporations, who have become some of the largest and most powerful in the world, program their AI to funnel the videos and articles most apt to reinforce the prejudices of the user and is suspected of manipulating search engine algorithms in order to "pre-edit" the information that people would find, or not find, in their searches in order to surreptitiously sway elections in a certain direction so in the case of social media these concerns have some evidence to back them up.

Between elections political parties are engaged in a constant process of manipulation and propaganda; they are always running for re-election. Their existence fosters a politics-as-war atmosphere that keeps these animosities active in the populace and never really lets things settle down. We accept this as inevitable and truth be told it can provide a certain level of drama and excitement to our lives, although as of late we could all use a bit less of that.

Although something akin to political parties would still exist under JD the power dynamics would be quite different from what we see in present day democracies. People have freedom of association and so would be able to create organizations in order to influence the public but these organizations would have no direct power to legislate as do political parties who win power in our present system. They would also not be able to influence legislation through donations to political candidates as there would be no candidates. The most they could do is to present ideas for legislation and promote them to the public in the hope that the ideas would gain traction with the citizenry and influence the decisions of which ever citizens get called for jury duty. One could imagine a great number of organizations competing for the ear of the public through all the means that are now used such as advertising, public relations, mass media, etc. This is an expected and healthy process in a democracy but, again, these organizations would have no direct power to legislate as our elected parties now have.

I will not, in this book, attempt to make a case for democracy as such. Although some of the greatest minds in western history have argued against democracy, this question has been settled in the affirmative for the vast majority of citizens in the West and significant numbers of people elsewhere. I also will not delve into strengths and weaknesses of the various other forms of democracy; all of them, except for "town hall" direct democracy which still exists in some small communities and those countries like Switzerland who conduct referendums, are various forms of representative democracy in which a person is elected to represent the constituents of a particular jurisdiction.

I am also not going to spill a great deal of ink making a case against politicians. They make that case themselves, hourly, daily, continuously. They stink up the atmosphere merely by existing. Nobody actually likes politicians, at least as a group, although most people are not so cynical as to condemn all of them. If we have been around for a while or read a few history books we can name a small number of them who were obviously possessed of good intentions and an actual desire to deliver genuine benefits to their constituents, and occasionally statesman of world historical significance who steps forth during times of great turmoil and with courageous and decisive action alters the course of the nation and sometimes the world as well. But for the most part, when surveying the field of candidates who present themselves to the voters for consideration one is reminded of filmmaker Eric Allen Bell's oh so apt description of these types as "sociopathic attention whores" A certain shamelessness seems to be a prerequisite for the job along with a certain level of acting skill which allows one to spout inane banalities as if something important is being said. We take these knaves so much for granted, as they are indeed necessary under representative democracy, that we fail to fully appreciate to what extent they degrade the moral tone of our societies. Although people do not generally think in these psycho-social terms I believe that looking up to the pinnacle of our culture to see these amoral, conniving, greedy, power- hungry individuals and realizing that these morally inferior people are our lords and masters is subtly but deeply disillusioning. We console ourselves that we are at least fortunate that we do not live under a totalitarian dictatorship as so many unfortunate people do, and believing such an arrangement is inevitable, shrug and go on about our lives and try to ignore them until the next election when we once again hold our nose and vote for the least unsavory of the lot.

Campaign Financing

Then there is the legalized bribery we refer to as campaign contributions. I will only say about such a system that it cannot be anything but corrupting. There are no disinterested donors and the politician better realize that if he hopes to prevail. But the citizenry should not have to pay any extra to the people they have already elected to do their jobs and should not have to put up with being out-bid by special interest groups.

Elections are very expensive and politicians solicit donations from as wide a selection of organizations and individuals as possible which is little more than a bidding war for political influence. This is probably the main reason for the great discrepancy between the desires of the majority and what the people actually receive. The politician suddenly changes his mind or proposes a bill that was not even mentioned during the campaign. This mystery is usually solved by checking the donor list and the amounts contributed.

Under JD any kind of bribery or influence peddling would be much more difficult as there are no politicians or parties to bribe and the jurors are randomly chosen. The entry point for corruption under JD would be to identify the jurors and try to bribe or intimidate them individually but there would be severe penalties for this practice for both parties and in cases where the stakes are high there could be secret juries making it as difficult as possible for bad actors to identify the juror. Or, interested parties could try to bribe bureaucrats directly. Again this is not possible to completely prevent but severe enough penalties would be a strong disincentive.

This is not just a practice where the virtuous politicians are corrupted by the evil businessman; it's a two-way street, a profitable dance in which both parties engage. The interested party does not always get what they want of course as there are many other interested parties and some decisions are scrutinized more then others but "pay-to-play" is just recognized by all parties as how things are done. It's much easier to get away with a particular move when the media is not paying attention either because they are uninterested or that they are incentivized not to pay attention, which is often the case. JD, by removing the politician from this formula, make it much more difficult for powerful forces to exert control. The juror is in a decision making role for only a brief period of time and then they are merely powerless citizens once again. How can this arrangement be gamed? The jury is also in control of the choice of experts to consult. They are under no obligation to kowtow to some bureaucratic regulator or another. They can ignore this person completely if they want, maybe even recommend that his position be re-evaluated if he gets pushy. Again, much harder to game.

A Brief Suggestion

For those jurisdictions that do not feel ready to experiment with such a radical change in their system as I am proposing, allow me to make a suggestion that I believe would dramatically improve any form of representative democracy now in existence.

I propose that the process of election financing be almost completely brought under government authority. Every established political party would be given by the government, which means by the taxpayer, an equal amount of money with which to finance their electoral run. Anyone, whether private citizen, corporation or anyone else would be subject to severe legal penalties for trying to offer any monies or incentives of any kind, to a political party or politician. Anyone caught doing so, whether on the receiving or contributing side would do serious prison time if caught. Notice I said "established" political party. A party would have to attract a significant percentage, say 10%, of the popular vote to qualify which would prevent just anyone from starting a political party in order to cash in. Any new or minor party would be allowed to raise money privately but would have to switch to the public financing system once they crossed the official threshold percentage. Elections would be financed by the taxpayer and not the rich and powerful who the politicians are incentivized to favour. A large multinational could still try to get its way by threatening to locate business in another jurisdiction or refusing to sell a product in the jurisdiction in question but removing the usual sources of private funds would dramatically incentivize politicians to pay much less attention to these special interest groups and more to the people.

This system is in my opinion not as good as juristical democracy as it can be gamed, at least in the short term; and no I'm not going to say how; the moneymen are going to have to figure that out on their own.

Involved Institutions

The three main institutions that I will include in my argument, aside from the executive branch itself would be corporations, bureaucracy and the media. Educational, scientific institutions and the military are also important but they do not have the same overwhelming and omnipresent quality of the big three mentioned above so my treatment of them will brief. Before examining these institutions I will first define this new system, which I call Juristical Democracy, and sketch out its basic structure and functions and then differentiate the ways that these institutions would interact with JD as opposed to the system of representative democracy.

A New Model

Juristical Democracy is designed to cut through all of the layers of obfuscation and bad-faith actors that thwart the will of the people and return the political decision making apparatus to ordinary citizens. It would bring political and economic decision making processes out of the corporate boardrooms and the back rooms of party-based politics down to the street level where the spirit of a proper democracy should live. Although it will take this book to explore the mechanisms of this system of democracy in some detail, the essence of the system is simplicity itself, which is that ***the jury system that we already use to decide the guilt or innocence of individuals or corporate bodies should be applied to the law making machinery of government itself.*** As we now put people and corporations on trial we should also put legislation on trial. The bills and legislation that are now decided by elected bodies should instead be put before a jury and be found worthy to be enacted into law or not, sent back to the sponsor to be modified or completely scrapped. The process that we now use in criminal trials of calling witnesses, or in this system, advocates, if you want to call them that, for the prosecution and defense, of cross-examination and rebuttal, with expert testimony on both sides, would be applied to the interrogation of the proposed bill or challenge to an existing law. This would, of course, profoundly alter the power dynamics of society in ways too numerous to fully predict and would be a risky leap into an uncertain future. But the future is uncertain now is it not?

JD takes democracy back from the elites; the bureaucrats, technocrats, capitalists, socialists and autocrats both global and local, the transnational organizations who have been captured, if they were never not captured, by often hostile actors, the giant faceless self-interested bureaucracies, the organized professional societies who are very good at engineering make-work projects for themselves at the expense of the public; what is the unemployment rate among doctors and lawyers? - the megalomaniacal dictators, call them fascist or communist, in the end it hardly matters. All of these organizations would still exist under JD, except the dictators hopefully, but they would all be under the regular scrutiny of the public via the JD mechanism who would have the authority to enact legislation, formulate public policy, hire and fire government personnel, recommend criminal charges, reform, create and shut down entire bureaucracies.

Juristical democracy is designed to replace representative democracy completely. There would be no politicians, no standing legislature, no senate, no congress, no mayors, no presidents or prime-ministers, no elected officials of any kind. There would be no divisive "party platforms" as there would be no political parties, no four year countdown with the increasing sense that "everything is on the line" in this election, as there would be no elections; no polarizing president for the opposite party to hate; no supreme court to stack with ideological compatriots. Democratic decisions would be piecemeal, focused more on the particulars of the case at hand rather on enacting grand ideological narratives or rewarding campaign donors.

There may on occasion be referendums on certain issues if a jury so decides, but regular periodic elections would not exist.

There would be national, provincial and municipal representatives who would also be chosen by juries to represent the country, province, state or city in political or business negotiations. They would be more accurately described as negotiators or diplomats. They would have absolutely no direct domestic power at all and their power to make binding decisions would be constrained by jury ratification. There would also be military leaders chosen from a pool of nominees by a process of interviews and biographical research.

Under JD the citizen would feel more involved in the running of his society. Even if he was never called for jury duty he would know that the laws under which he is governed would be the creation of ordinary people like him instead of a technocratic elite who are inevitably imbedded in or influenced by a ruling class. In our present democracy anyone can run for office in theory but in practice almost anyone who wins an election is either a part of the present moneyed elite or compromised by them as in order to mount a campaign they must raise vast sums of money from donors who certainly want much in return. And because the politically powerful are either from a wealthy background or, through influence peddling, will soon be wealthy, they find it difficult to even understand the lives of ordinary people. JD puts ordinary people in charge. A random sampling of citizens will intuitively embody the zeitgeist of a society far better than cadres of siloed elites.

One of the great advantages of Juristical Democracy is that a large number of issues can be dealt with simultaneously by the public whereas under our representative system only a small number of issues can be brought before the public at any one time. Elections often turn on a single issue with most of the other issues, many of great import, being dealt with by an anonymous and unelected bureaucracy with their own agendas. The public often first hears of a issue only after a decision has already been made and is in the process of being enacted and unless there is a public outcry sufficiently large enough to embarrass the politician into reconsidering their decision the bureaucratic wheels just keep on turning. This hidden machinery of the state would become more explicit under JD with the citizens involved at every level excluding some military matters which must be kept secret for national security reasons and high-level diplomatic negotiations in which trust must be put into the hands of negotiators and not micro-managed.

Juristical democracy would profoundly change the authoritarian dynamic of society. There would still be institutional authority but it would be experienced more as a bottom-up emanation of the popular will rather than a submission to the will of a remote and often invisible elite who have become accountable to too many interested parties apart from the electorate that they are intended to serve.

People under this system would know at a very deep level that their society reflected, most of all, the priorities and concerns of ordinary, fairly average individuals instead of a tiny minority of ideologues or the rich or the globalists and multinational corporations. Not that the interests of these groups would not be taken into account as being wealthy, or a senior bureaucrat or a corporate CEO or even an ideologue does not mean that one does not have a valuable contribution to make, just that in the modern world where wealth is power, the influence of such people is excessive and often not beneficial to anyone but themselves. Decisions would be made in a democratic and transparent manner and not the present corrupt and secretive "smoke filled room" way. The people would experience a more intimate sense of ownership of the social order rather than experiencing themselves as victims of external forces. However they would also simultaneously feel more responsible when things went wrong. They would not be able to blame "those damn politicians" anymore but would have to own any mistakes made and take responsibility for fixing them which encouraged a more responsible and adult mentality in the citizenry. I want to make it clear that juristical democracy does not romanticize the judgement of the people. Juries will make mistakes because humans are fallible and mistakes are inevitable. The virtue is in the jury system itself. The randomness of the jury selection process prevents power factions from developing because, in a paradoxical way, no-one is in charge and everyone is in charge. It allows, actually demands, that the jurors think much more deeply about any given issue than most of them would under our present representative democratic system where they are only ever given a chance to exercise choice every four or five years when they pick their favorite sound bite to vote on and for the particular megalomaniac that they hope will screw them over the least.

But, you might ask, isn't this all much too complicated for a juror who might have only a high school education? How can they possibly evaluate complex political or scientific issues. But they already decide on these issues indirectly by voting for one politician or another who presents these issues to the electorate for consideration. Citizens are considered competent enough to serve on criminal juries with serious, often life and death consequences for the individual involved. The jury system would actually allow the citizen the time and resources to examine the issues in far more depth than they normally would and without having to contend with the bias of the media and the news cycle format of edited interviews and slick talking-heads spinning the issue in service of their paymasters. Every jury would be able to hire, at taxpayers expense, qualified experts in the field relevant to the issue being evaluated to explain and advise them. If at the end of the process they still feel unable to come to a decision regarding the legislation they may defer to the experts although the final decision would always be up to the jury and not the expert. If jurors decide if an individual should be incarcerated or in some jurisdictions, to live or die, then why can't they decide if a particular piece of legislation should live or die? In criminal trials expert witnesses are called and the process is monitored by a judge but in the end we trust the judgement of the jury. This system is not that different in this respect. As far as the judges go it would be a good idea to get rid of this position altogether as the judge can be seen as merely an elitist voice trying to impose so-called enlightened opinion upon the jury by controlling procedure and protocol, although there may be a legal consultant or consultants, chosen by the jury of course, who might be called upon for advice. As mentioned before each jury can hire a guide or expert on the issue at hand and if a juror feels that the decision is beyond his competence he can defer to the expert for a decision although the expert can never be allowed to forcibly override the jury. Using terminology from moviemaking, the juror always gets final cut. This system of democracy fuses educated expertise with the common sense of the citizen who after all has a vested interest in the smooth functioning of the community and country in which he lives. It also prevents, as much as is practical, the system being hijacked by a self-interested cabal of experts as the expert in question is chosen by the juror and not appointed by some authority who may very well be under the influence of the previously mentioned cabal. Experts who complain of the difficulties of explaining difficult technical concepts to jurors are just going to have to up their game. Every field has at least a few people with a talent for popularizing technical and scientific ideas in a reasonably accurate way. The skills and ideas that would go into cultivating a good juror should be part of the educational system and could be started at a young age with mock juries drawn up in the classroom. Critical thinking skills, sound techniques for gathering evidence, instruction in statistical analysis, interrogating witnesses and drawing good conclusions would be taught. Classes could go on field trips to observe real juries in action.

This would obviously be a revolutionary new way of governing and one would reasonably have concern as to how to transition from a normal representative form of government. I would offer two suggestions. One would be to start with the smaller political jurisdictions with a lower level of complexity such as municipal, state and provincial governments and then later transition to the national level. At the national level one could start with one branch of the government and once JD was operating for a while and one could see how it functioned then a country could decide if they wanted to go all in.

Choosing the Issues

Anyone can present an issue for the jury, from the largest worldwide institution such as the Catholic Church or the United Nations or the government of another country, to some random individual who has scribbled a question on the back of a napkin while he was drunk at the pub. They can be e-mails or a verbal proposal recorded on YouTube. Anything goes.

It is obvious that there will be many submissions of a great range of quality. It can be a long, very detailed, scientifically referenced, multi-volume opus; the main problem would be to get the jury to consider it. They may simply take a look at the great beast and decide to take a pass. So be it, there are no guarantees in this process. There should *not* be a permanent bureaucracy whose job it is to choose the issues as this bureaucracy would be vulnerable to takeover by interested factions of one sort or another. The body responsible should just be a preliminary jury randomly chosen from the voter rolls as is the case for ordinary criminal or civil juries. One of the main rationales for the system of juristical democracy is to prevent any kind of permanent power factions from forming. It should be seen as a kind of random generator for the expression of the spirit or zeitgeist of a particular society in its engagement with an ever-changing world.

If a person's submission is not chosen the person may submit it again although limits will have to be put in place as to how many submissions will be allowed in a certain period of time in order to prevent the usual kooks and saboteurs from swamping the system.

One should avoid interference by bureaucrats except perhaps at the very beginning of the process as there would have to be a storage and sorting process where proposals are received and collated for perusal by the preliminary jury. This would be a centralized repository and/or website. A physical repository might be preferred as with a website there would be a temptation to astroturf the site thus making an issue seem more urgent that it would otherwise be but in our online world there would no doubt be a place for a web based repository as well as this would give an opportunity for citizens in more remote areas to make their voices heard. Care must be taken with the staffing of a repository and the protocols in place for sorting and storage as it would be vulnerable to interference by interested parties who might accidentally drop a proposal into the trash, never to be seen again.

Characteristics of the Jury

The modern citizen in the 21st century in many ways lives in the most complex and confusing information environment in history. Dozens of TV channels, Tik Tok, facebook, UTube, etc., constant interruptions from the smartphone, it goes on and on. It surely is a great ball of confusion and one of the main problems with modern democracy is the practical difficulties of the citizen finding the time and also knowing where to find the relevant data to research the issues involved. There is usually a continuous stream of issues zipping by with a few being paid attention to in any systematic manner. In fact you can say that it is virtually impossible to do so, the issues being so numerous and so technical and complex. The citizen just can't keep up. JD is meant to counteract this problem. A group of citizens are chosen, perhaps for the first and only time in their lives and they are asked to focus in depth on one issue only, and are given the time and resources which they could not marshal by themselves; qualified experts, facilities for research, travel resources, etc, and are encouraged to discuss and debate the issues under consideration. They are given a sanctuary that allows them to step back from the usual media driven confusion and the pressures and distractions of everyday life and explore an issue in depth.

One significant change in this process over a criminal trial would be the right of the jury members to do much more than just listen and take notes. They would take a very active role in the process, asking questions, doing their own research, travelling to relevant locations to explore things first-hand, even commissioning new research depending on the requirements of the situation. The jurors could even begin their research before they are formally called to join the other jurors in their task.

Except in case of an emergency most jurors would be informed of being called to jury duty several weeks or months before having to show up so they can make arrangements with their employer and family to accommodate their task. There is no reason that, except in cases of classified material, that they cannot be given the information on the issue under consideration and could begin their own research and/or discussions with others if they so wish. This should be encouraged as it would give the juror time to clarify the issue in his mind and formulate questions and/or objections to take into the official jury process in order to discuss with other jurors. It would also be permissible in most cases to allow jurors to communicate with each other before the official trial begins. Ideas could be bounced around, books recommended, potential consultants considered so that the juror would come to trial with certain questions already in mind. Jurors would be encouraged to ask questions and discuss the issues throughout the process rather than only at the end of it as would happen in a criminal trial. The process would be far more freewheeling than a criminal trial and sequestering jurors or mandating that jurors not be allowed to communicate any details about the case to anyone else would only be relevant in cases where national security is an issue. Jurors could discuss the matter with the wider community if they wished so as to get a better sense of the issue at the street level. An individual's life or freedom is not at stake and no legal precedents are being set so there is no need to be as rigidly scrupulous. Precedents can be completely ignored in juristical democracy; this is a populist, from the ground up political system; common law precedent is not relevant to the process in any formal way as it is in criminal trials as one would assume that the decisions of multiple juries over time would inevitably reflect the common will of the people. Also, the jury can, as part of their decision, mandate a periodic review of the results of any decision to assess its efficacy.

A Hierarchy of Juries

A Multi-level Jury System

There would, in most cases, be three levels of juries; the preliminary, the main and the final juries but in some cases there might be only one level of jury and in other cases up to four levels. A multiple level jury system works in a similar way as the "branches of government" model to provide checks and balances to the decision making process. The final jury exists to decide if the decision of the main jury gets passed into law.

The number of juries needed to evaluate an issue would depend on the particular decision under consideration and the budgetary and time considerations of the particular community. Smaller communities may choose to employ only one level of jury for the process. There could be neighborhood juries whose purview would only extend to a particular block or blocks or even street; every place that people live has informally recognized neighborhoods that could form their own juries. Then there are formally recognized incorporated jurisdictions like villages, towns, cities, states, provinces and countries.

For example a small town or village may be trying to decide to place a traffic light at an intersection as there has been a number of collisions at this location and a consensus has developed that something should be done about it. It is obvious that this is considered an important issue by the majority of the community members and it should not be necessary to go through the time and expense of using a preliminary or final jury for this process. A single jury would do. The informal consensus of smaller communities is much easier to decipher than for larger communities. There would be fewer potential issues that would arise and therefore less need for the preliminary jury which exists mostly to prioritize issues and set the parameters of the main jury. Setting parameters for the main jury would not be necessary for such a straightforward decision. Larger towns, cities, provinces and nations would employ three levels of jury and possibly four if it would be preferred that the preliminary jury that chose the issues to be considered be separate from the preliminary jury whose job it would be to set parameters for the main jury.

The Preliminary Jury

The preliminary jury's task is to choose the issue to be adjudicated by the main jury and also to set the parameters of the main jury depending on the complexity and specific characteristics of the issue. Parameters could include jury size, educational restrictions, regions from which the jury members could be chosen from to prevent jurisdictional favoritism, which consultants might be useful to include. It would also set budgets and deadlines. It would stay intact until the main jury came to a decision as the main jury may request more time or resources.

The preliminary jury would be the first level and larger communities would have any number of preliminary juries functioning simultaneously as there would be more issues being presented for consideration. The importance of the issue would help determine the number of jurors chosen to serve on the main jury. Fairly minor issues would require a smaller number of jurors whereas major issues would be best decided by larger juries. The particulars of the issue at hand would also factor into the decision whether to exclude particular individuals from serving on the jury if they have a significant financial or other interest in the outcome of the decision although the preliminary jury could encourage or even nominate the excluded party to be consulted by the main jury during their research phase of the process. The degree of unanimity would also be set by the preliminary jury with a higher degree of unanimity required depending on the importance of the issue and the severity of the possible outcomes of the decisions. The expense of paying the jurors would also be a factor and the smaller the community the more that monetary considerations for both juror compensation and compensation for expert advisors would come under consideration. Juries at the national level where the issue is especially consequential as in whether to go to war for example or to substantially overhaul the medical system, the jury could be especially large. There is no really objective way to set the number of jurors required but it would make sense that the more important and consequential the decision the more it would make sense to have a larger jury as the more jurors voting, the more of a chance that the decision would more accurately reflect the perspective of the general population. Larger juries would only make sense for the main jury as they would be doing the vast majority of the work. The preliminary and final juries could have a more traditional number of jurors as is common in criminal trials. There would, of course, be an allowance for an appeal process due to unforeseen complexities in the evaluation process but the main jury would have to make its case each time to the preliminary jury for any extension that it might request. The preliminary jury could also recommend names of experts in various fields and where to find such individuals although the final decision on whom to consult would be up to the members of the main jury.

The Main Jury

The main jury would be performing the main part of the task of evaluating the issue to be legislated upon, hence its name. It would look more like an informal classroom of equals, which is exactly what it would be, rather than the highly controlled situation that is found in criminal trials where competing lawyers and a judge adjudicate via a complex formal process where every move is highly procedural and controlled. This is totally proper during a criminal trial of course but would not be necessary during a legislative trial. Jurors could work as a complete group with all the other members present or split off into smaller groups to research different aspects of the case or work on the research process at an individual level. They could regroup as a whole to evaluate their progress as many times as they wanted during the process at which point they could further decide what specific further steps should be taken to come to a decision.

The whole group could be mandated to meet together when experts are called as consultants or the various stakeholders involved in the field or industry to be legislated upon are presenting their arguments but individuals could form into any configuration that they wanted to do further research. There would be no limitations on what source material could be allowed into the process; books, scientific studies, polls, the internet, personal consults with any and all individuals that the juror sees fit to talk to including travelling to any location to examine the facts on the ground or talk to anyone who, for one reason or another, could or would not come into the courtroom. Jurors would not be required to keep any information from each other or any opinions to themselves but would be encouraged to share and discuss anything they wanted at any time with other jurors. It would even be permitted to conduct public polls either in-person or by phone or even via social media if time permits in order to gauge the public regarding their views or mood regarding a particular issue. In other words there would be no source of information that would be off limits unless it would endanger national security or would violate some individuals right to privacy.

The Final Jury

The final jury would be tasked with the responsibility of ratifying the decision of the main jury and passing the new legislation into law. If a certain percentage of the jurors do not agree with the decision they can send it back to the main jury for reevaluation with the relevant critiques and suggestions attached. A certain amount of back and forth would be permitted between the main and final jury but if the legislation is formally rejected more than twice the process should be considered a failure. This will guard against the danger of a particularly incompetent jury, which statistically is bound to happen, from committing serious errors or, under the sway of a charismatic or bullying member, submitting to groupthink. A new main jury could be struck to repeat the process or if the issue is deemed sufficiently important a vote could be taken to present the issue to the public for a referendum.

The final jury would need the least amount of time and resources and would not be expected to consult experts or do any in-depth research. It might take only a short time to reject or ratify.

Jury Groups

Especially complex decisions may take several phases involving multiple juries before any definitive decision would take place. The main jury might decide that certain questions must be answered before any more progress can be made. It would pass this on to the final jury which, if it agreed, would strike another preliminary jury which would set a timeline where the interested parties would have the opportunity to revise their submission. The interested parties could apply to the jury to commission a poll or study to obtain more information or clarify and issue if required. So aside from the preliminary, main and final jury triad there could be a series of jury groups forming and dissolving and involving multiple steps until any final decision is made. Jury groups should only be needed where large bureaucracies were being reformed as many questions may need to be studied independently before any final decision is made.

Parameters of the Jury

The parameters of the main jury would be set by the preliminary jury. They would be the best combination of standards and characteristics required for the jurors to come to a good decision. They would choose from a database of eligible citizens categorized by various criteria such as age, educational level, occupation, profession or any other criterion that the jury considered relevant. The potential jurors would be interviewed by the preliminary jury and either accepted or rejected for duty. The importance of the issue along with any unique characteristics of the issue under judgement would be the relevant factors in this decision. An issue involving a high degree of scientific and technical complexity would lead the jury to select for a higher level of education than a more straightforward common-sense type of issue which would require that the jury consider fewer variables, perhaps only an age and citizenship requirement.

This means that only the preliminary and final juries are always randomly chosen from a list of eligible citizens. The main jury does most of the actual work of researching the issue and interviewing witnesses and consultants and where narrower parameters would be justified depending on the technical requirements of the process. An objection could be raised here that since qualified experts are already being consulted that there is no need to set juror standards any higher than one would in randomly choosing the preliminary jury. It would depend on the degree of complexity of the issue and there is no neat way to set the parameters here. There are many different levels of complexity possible and the average citizen might not have the intellectual or educational standards to even begin to evaluate the recommendations of the experts being consulted so higher than average standards may have to be set for the main jury. These might include academic standards with anything from an undergraduate science degree or an engineering degree, the passing of aptitude or IQ tests, a certain number of years of work experience in a certain field, etc. It would be good for lists of potential jurors to already be categorized according to some of these parameters which could be done starting before they reach age eligibility and thereafter the individual could add any additional educational credential earned to his profile. As counter to the objection that I am smuggling in elitism here by setting higher standards for the main jury and violating one of the basic premises of JD, remember that their decision must be ratified by the final jury which would be a broad based random jury and not as specialized as the main jury. The final jury would be the common sense "sniff test" that the new legislation would have to pass.

Another question that should be considered as important, and might even be set by law, would be parameters set to limit jury participation to persons, even in preliminary and final juries, who would have a higher level of maturity, responsibility and life experience than a randomly chosen individual. Maturity, responsibility and life experience are not characteristics that can be quickly evaluated, we can say they are not the same as educational level or high expertise, but a few rough heuristics would be age, family status and years of residence in a jurisdiction.

Our mid 20's is roughly the age when most of us begin to emerge from the cloud of hormonally induced insanity that begins at the onset of puberty, and there is no single event that grows you up like having children. Children help inculcate a consciousness of the future; the long term health of your society becomes even more real as a consequence of having them, so a minimum age of 25, married and with children would be a good base criterion.

Restricting jury duty for recent newly minted citizens also makes sense. A person should have lived in a jurisdiction for several years at least before they would be considered qualified to pass judgement on most issues under consideration. A 25 year old juror who immigrated into the country at age 10 would be preferable to one who arrived at age 20. A 10 year old still has that sponge-like ability to absorb cultural mores at an intuitive level much more than a 20 year old and would be expected to have a much more intimate understanding of the culture than someone who immigrates in their late teens or later. Of course the total number of years of residence matters as well. By the time the 20 year-old immigrant reaches middle-age they can be expected to have attained a reasonably good sense of the zeitgeist of their adopted country. I just use these examples to point out that this issue should be given consideration.

As this statement illustrates JD is not a form of universal democracy. A certain percentage of the population is unfit to be making these important decisions and for reasons that may not be quantifiable as reflected in their level of education or life or job experience. With some people you can just smell the crazy coming off them; they might, on paper, seem an ideal candidate for service but something seems off, which is why the preliminary jury should never have to justify its vetting process to anyone. Reason matters, but so does intuition.

Experts

We live in the age of the expert. There have always been experts of course. Even in the most primitive societies one looked to designated individuals for guidance whether this be the shaman or an experienced herbalist or midwife, those people who had apprenticed with a learned elder to master whatever craft or activity that was of value to the tribe. Even until quite recently, when the great majority of our ancestors still lived a rural agrarian existence, expertise was something one attained by working alongside parents and extended family members and learning by informal observation and experience. The professional expert who was formally trained and worked for money existed but there was much less of a need for them in a technologically simpler age when most of the problems were simpler and could be addressed informally and locally. But increasingly, starting from the scientific and industrial revolutions the world has become much more complex with the principle of the division of labour and increasing specialization rendering the traditional "jack of all trades" effectively extinct. With the increase in scientific experimental technologies the level of education required to qualify for expertise increased, along with a specialized technical language required to communicate with one's colleagues. So, this specialization was a natural and necessary development driven by the vast amounts of new knowledge discovered over the past several centuries. But this also made the fields of study increasingly inaccessible to ordinary people and required an increasing faith in both the expert and the societal filtering mechanism (i.e. the media and educational system) which reported the theories and findings of the experts to the public but these layers of selection and reporting along with the increasing amounts of money required to finance the studies introduced many ways that the process could be distorted and corrupted.

An aspect of the media that is especially germane in this time of the Covid-19 pandemic is the relationship between the media and the expert class if I may call them that or maybe expert classes would be more accurate as there are many types of expertise. The types of experts in the media hot seat depends on what is considered by the viewers to be most important at any one time. I believe that the three-way relationship between the media, the politicians and the expert class is most problematic at this point in time and perhaps at any time

It would be wise to pay closer attention to the relationship between the expert and the media, politicians and corporations. Politicians select experts that give them a rationale for greater power and control. The media select experts for shock value and to promote the experts who align with the ideology of the particular publication in question. Corporations select experts whose conclusions align with their financial interests. They can also influence the "consensus" by financing the agreeable experts and, since they own the studies, choose not to publish results that they do not like. The more money and power at stake in the conclusions of the expert the more of a incentive for interested parties to select the expert shift the narrative in their favour

We are constantly admonished to "follow the science" and to "trust the science" and told that "the science is settled". But what is "the science"? Is it just what the scientists say? What if scientists say different things? How do you decide which one to follow, ask another scientist? Besides the scientific consensus is only the opinion of the majority of experts in a certain field at a certain time and as history shows, the consensus has been shown to be wrong on many occasions so the prudent attitude is to always be at least somewhat skeptical of scientific consensus at any point in time. Scientists are often quite wrong about things and if this is so then how much should we trust them? How does an ordinary citizen decide?

Why should you trust the media to present the best experts? Do they not have an incentive to sensationalize rather that present the proper nuance? Does this not incentivize the expert who is more interested in attention more that truth?

Is not the expert who is more interested in personal empire building willing to shade the truth to gain access to positive media coverage and government or corporate money?

That the juror always gets to override the expert changes the power dynamic in several ways. It forces experts to speak in a way that the citizenry understands. The expert just cannot say "I am taking over this process and imposing my decision on you the jury by fiat because I'm the expert and you are not; I have the qualifications and you don't". The citizen always gets final say no matter what and without having to justify himself to the expert. The juror will sometimes find, in his investigations, that the "scientific consensus" is often a mirage manufactured by the scientific-bureaucratic-corporate complex in the service of vast financial and bureaucratic interests and that "peer-review" is often a system of mutual back-scratching; a pretentious cover for scientific conformity.

Expert consultants can be questioned individually or real time debates can be arranged between experts with opposing viewpoints as contradictions and weak arguments are often best revealed in the messy back and forth of a debate rather than in a more formal venue where presentations are often highly curated.

Bureaucracy

The problem of bureaucracy is and will always be a vexing one for any regime no matter what form that regime takes. National level bureaucracies are huge behemoths often having hundreds of thousands of employees and although, technically, bureaucrats are "public servants" they are, as are all humans not striving for sainthood, self-centered beings who are pursuing their own interests whether they are aware of this or not. Senior bureaucrats should be seen as CEO's running a non-profit business; in fact their position is even more enviable than a CEO of a for-profit enterprise who has to take in at least as much money as they spend. The senior bureaucrat is under much less pressure to come in under budget; he can apply to the head of state for a bigger slice of the pie at any time and is in fact under pressure to spend 100% of his annual budget whether this is warranted or not so as to avoid having his budget cut in the next year. There is always the incentive to invent new mandates at the drop of a hat which are often nothing but make-work projects invented to please the employees and their political masters. And the senior bureaucrat who is heading up a bureaucracy is usually quite aware of his comparative status among the other CEO's heading up all the other bureaucracies in the government. Whereas a CEO in private industry measures his status by market share and total earnings the government bureaucrat measures his status by how much tax money he can control and spend. If his budget is increased from the previous year he considers himself more successful even if the policies of the bureaucracy he heads are in fact impoverishing his country and harming the people that he is supposedly trying to help. The size and expense of his bureaucracy might have little to do with the real world needs that the bureaucracy was expected to solve or the results obtained might at one time have been needed but times have changed and since the bureaucracy is decoupled from market incentives it can just continue on with its often increasingly destructive trajectory. The politician avoids confronting the organization as the bureaucrats both votes in elections and are responsible for enacting legislation and may use all manner of delaying and obfuscatory tactics if they do not like the politicians policies. Juristical democracy removes this first incentive as there is no politician to vote for or to thwart or please. There may still be forms of passive-aggressive obstructionist behavior on the part of the bureaucracy toward any legislative decision arrived at by the jury and there is no simple answer as to how this would be dealt with but a couple of points could be raised in this matter. One is that ordinary citizens, who would be the members of the jury, generally hold an attitude of well deserved resentment toward government employees as said employees are often over-compensated financially and in receipt of perks and privileges that often far exceed what their private sector counterparts get for an equivalent effort. Another factor is that under JD senior bureaucrats would be appointed by a group of citizen jurors rather than a head of state which would mean that the usual elitist old boys network attitude that often underpins these appointments would be severely weakened. A preliminary jury could also exclude bureaucrats and any or all government employees from even serving on juries including judges, lawyers, police, military or anyone else who derives the main of their income from the government on the principle that they would have a higher than average incentive to vote in a self-interested manner than a citizen in the private sector. But the main advantage is that a jury would have the right at any time to demand that any bureaucrat at any level have their behavior and position evaluated and behavior penalized up to and including termination of employment. And as for the political party hack appointments? No political parties, no problem.

Then there is the well documented phenomenon of senior employees of a bureaucracy being drawn from the senior ranks of the industry being "regulated". This is common enough that it is tempting to view it as merely a profitable business strategy. University of Chicago economist George Stigler recognized the practice, calling it "regulatory capture" or capture theory back in the 1970's. Interested, very wealthy industries have the time and resources to influence the regulatory bodies that set up self-serving regulations that are supposed to protect public health, environment. etc., whereas the ordinary citizen has a life to live and expects the politicians to protect his interests in such matters when they often do not. A policy of prohibiting people from moving back and forth between the corporate and bureaucratic worlds would be a sound idea in order to prevent such a confusion of agendas.

Add to this the innumerable NGO's and non-profits that have grown up over the past few decades. These barely register on the political landscape as players although they often work hand-in-glove with political parties to accomplish tasks that cannot for various reasons be allowed for the parties to do directly. They could be considered a kind of shadow bureaucracy at least in part.

The problem with establishing mandates and a bureaucracy to enact them is that the mandate sets in motion a process that is very difficult to stop even if the new policies start causing negative, often very negative, effects. The bureaucracy must justify it's existence and is in a sense obliged to fulfil it's mandate no matter if it is done competently or not. There is the very real risk that any science or expertise that is used to justify these mandates becomes co-opted and corrupted by the bureaucracy. Remember, to a politician, politics comes first which means the desires of the bureaucracy and political donors come first. After all the bureaucrats have to justify their position and their will always be scientists who gain much more satisfaction as one of the managerial elites with all the perks and privileged this entails than just being another anonymous researcher. Under JD bureaucratic mandates would be from a jury rather than a political party and would have built-in review timelines and self-destruct mechanisms in case things did not work out as planned, which, given the indeterminate nature of the real world would be more often than not. JD would give a jury the power to evaluate, discipline and replace senior bureaucrats including bringing in a complete outsider to shake things up. Juries would have the power to shut down entire bureaucracies if they so decided.

An Example of Bureaucratic Corruption

I will use as an illustration of the unfortunate real-world results of the corruption and back door politicking that characterizes our representative style of democracy an example that anyone in the English speaking world can relate to which is the food pyramid, introduced by the US Department of Agriculture in 1991 and replaced in 2011, as a guide for the citizenry to use to make sound nutritional choices.

Starting in the 1970's and accelerating through the 1980's the average weight for Americans rose quite dramatically. You can see it happen before your eyes if you watch crowd scenes from a few movies and also TV dramas and news programs from that era. You can see people packing on the pounds decade by decade. It's quite dramatic. People during and before the 70's are quite lean by todays standards and then get progressively heavier decade by decade. Not so much the stars who are paid to stay lean but the extras, the people in the crowd and background scenes.

It was obvious that the Big Four Food Group guidelines that had been in force since 1956 was showing it's age. It had been formulated to prevent deficiency diseases in an often undernourished population that had recently been subject to wartime rationing and to whom the great depression was still an often scarring memory. In a population with a low level of obesity and still living memories of scarcity this was good advice. But times had changed and so had Americans waistlines and this was accompanied by increases in the chronic diseases that inevitably accompany increases in bodyweight so the emphasis had to shift from "plenty of everything" to prevent deficiencies to a diet designed to nourish but with a greater focus on avoiding the more calorie dense, fattening foods. A more delicate balance had to be struck between nourishment and caloric restraint. The task was given to a nutritionist from New York University named Luise Light who assembled a team, who, after several months of research came out with guidelines designed to address the increasingly serious problems of obesity related chronic disease. It was a solid set of guidelines recommending plenty - 5 to 9 servings - of fresh fruits and vegetables, chock full of important micronutrients; moderate levels of fat and protein and very restricted levels of sugar and refined carbohydrates, i.e. junk food, which provide calories without much nutrition but also surprisingly restricted quantities of whole grain products which were limited to 2-3 servings a day which seems shockingly low considering the eventual 6-11 servings recommended in the final guide. How those grain servings went from 2-3 servings to 6-11 servings is illustrative of the dishonest and dare I say traitorous way that such an important public policy issue as the nutritional recommendations for an entire nation came to be. As the brilliant book "Death by Food Pyramid" by Denise Minger showed, the sensible and balanced recommendations of Light's team came back altered beyond recognition. The servings of grain products had been nearly quadrupled with no distinction, which Light's team had made, between whole and highly processed grains, fresh fruits and vegetables were cut from 5-9 down to 2-3 daily servings, which was only increased later due to an outcry from the National Cancer Institute. The reason given to Light for these changes was that poor people on food stamps would be better able to stay within their budget if they consumed more cheap carbohydrates than fresh vegetables which is true but would still mean they would eating a diet which would be much higher in empty calories and lower in the disease fighting nutrients found in those vegetables. The powers that be might have had to consider upping food stamp payments a few dollars a week to allow this and this was no doubt a complication they did not want to consider so they allowed an inferior, fattening, carbohydrate-heavy diet to be fobbed of onto the public instead. Light suspected however that the food stamp argument was more an excuse that a reason and according to Minger's investigation she was right. Minger uncovered evidence of interference from various agricultural pressure groups who were not happy with the recommended quantities of their particular agricultural product in Light's guidelines. Their lobbyists had a little chat with the politicians, drawing their attention no doubt to the generous contributions being shuffled into their campaign war chests. And so a nutritionally inferior carbohydrate heavy diet in which processed food was given priority over fresh, whole foods, potato chips were not differentiated from fresh potatoes and starchy grain servings were quadrupled to please the wheat and corn industries. Light's team protested that these levels of carbohydrates would lead to an epidemic of obesity and diabetes which turned out to be correct but the fix was in and Americans and those countries who followed their leads had their health sacrificed to the special corporate interests who managed to influence the politicians. In the conflict between the nutritionists and the food producers the food producers won, demonstrating that the USDA food pyramid was more about serving the economic interests of the food industry rather than the nutritional and health interests of the citizenry.

Also, the revision of Light's recommendations omitted the recommended 4 tablespoons of fat daily from her guidelines and succumbed to the new low-fat dogma recently gaining traction. The low-fat and low cholesterol bias came from other sources than the farm lobby, mainly the work of nutritional researcher Ancel Keys which purported to demonstrate a link between saturated fat and cholesterol consumption and heart disease and do-gooder politicians like George McGovern who had become personally enamored of the super low-fat Pritikin Diet and decided that it gave him the right to inflict his preferences on everyone else. But it conveniently reinforced the high-carb recommendations because when fats are stripped from the diet, flavour goes with it, and since one needs to find some enjoyment in life, new nutritional recommendations that include not only tons of carbs but does not distinguish between whole grain and refined, often sweetened carbs, is an officially approved way to consume high quantities of sugar sweetened foods to replace the flavour previously provided by fats. And just remember that the low cholesterol nonsense was repeated by the public health establishment for about 50 years -—not 5 years -—- 50; and has only in recent years been admitted to be in error which only goes to show you how longer one can persist in error when giant bureaucracies get pointed in the wrong direction, and when margarine manufacturers (no cholesterol!) provide funding for public health establishments.

In reality people kept their fat consumption about the same but consumed more high carb food thus increasing total calories, and their waistlines. The new recommendations allowed them to do it guilt free because they had been given the impression by slippery advertising, dodgy science and the new government approved pyramid that fat makes you fat and carbs not so much and so they could indulge guilt-free in those low-fat, zero-fat high sugar snack foods that flooded the market in the latter part of the 20th century.

Taking into account the revelations from Minger's book, the food pyramid and also the subsequent guidelines, rather than be seen as a font of health promoting information, the pyramid should itself have been slapped with a public health warning.

And to reiterate my point about dodgy science and to show that nothing has really been learned there is the Academy of Nutrition and Dietetics being sponsored by General Mills, PepsiCo, Kellogg's, Mars, Hershey's and the National Dairy Council and The Sugar Association. If you think that these companies do not exert influence over the public policies of the Academy then I have a bridge to sell you.

Corporations

Taken collectively corporations are the largest employer in the culture although no single corporation comes close to the number of employees represented by all levels of government although there are many multi-national corporations who are wealthier that a number of smaller countries. This gives them enormous influence over the economy and the government no matter what political system, short of full-on communism, that exists. Aside from the legalized briery known as campaign financing, corporations can always use the location of production facilities to discipline the various politicians and governments to negotiate an advantageous deal for themselves such as tax breaks. Steps can be taken however to incentivize corporations to remain in certain jurisdictions and this would be more likely to happen if the citizens of that jurisdiction were in charge of the process rather than the usual political operators. JD cannot prevent this tactic but at least one can be certain that some politicians "foundation" is not receiving donations or a politician and his party is accepting truck-loads of money for their campaign war chest and which would go a long way to assuring that regulatory decisions would have a greater chance of benefiting the citizenry.

There would be no universal policy on the type or level of regulations imposed on corporations under a particular political jurisdiction. This would evolve over time and in response to the particular political culture involved and the desires and needs of the population and the characteristics of the particular industry under consideration. Smaller, more local businesses would have different needs than large multinational ones. JD is designed to develop culturally specific solutions regarding the political economy.

Towns, cities and countries are all different from each other so top-down cookie-cutter solutions should not be expected. How a particular nation sees itself and how it fits into the world economy would naturally differ from another nation. The particular nation's culture, history, geography, resources, demographics and vision for itself would, over the decades and resulting from hundreds and thousands of jury decisions, result in a unique social order unlike any other nation. There is no universal culture and we should not expect there to be. There may be international alliances based on certain shared values and desired economic benefits but imposing a universal political order, liberal or otherwise, on the world is a mistake. Liberal imperialism is still imperialism; the pretense of liberal neutrality is just that, a pretense. Besides, imposing liberalism is rather self-contradictory is it not? In the couple of cases where it has worked well, which would be Germany and Japan after WW2, both nations had been completely crushed militarily and had unconditionally surrendered. No, liberal countries, if they want to be ambassadors for liberalism, must lead by example and hope that other countries see the benefits in adopting liberal values and we should accept the fact that some cultures might decide otherwise.

The Media

Trying to understand the world through the media is like looking at the world through a straw. What is revealed is merely a slice, and quite a thin slice, of reality at large. We have been immersed in television based media for about 70 years now when the nightly news began being beamed into the populations living rooms on a mass scale. It's difficult to get any kind of objective perspective on our relationship with it as it has been so omnipresent for so long. It is difficult in the 21st century to find any group of people so remote as to have been deprived of this experience and so to provide a control group. The Amish perhaps but they live in a culture so very different from the main that it is difficult to make any solid comparisons. And the introduction of computer driven media and now smartphones leaves us with a world where it could be said that we all have minds that have merged, at some sense, with this radically new and unprecedented technology. The medium itself responds to the many desires of both the public consumers of the media, the media owners, the advertisers, journalists, producers and consultants all which may have conflicting interests. The most important issue for our purposes here would be the veracity of the news and how completely it reflected the many and varied perspectives of the bulk of the populace. At this point in history we are witnessing the replacement of the old model of a relatively small handful of television news networks, newsmagazines and newspapers with a veritable wild west show of online social media. To call the situation chaotic is to engage in gross understatement with the old style media attempting to remain relevant by engaging in practices that increasingly violate the old-school "fair and balanced" ethical ideals. AI algorithms do not select for the traditional ideals but funnel information to the user that reinforce and strengthen previous prejudices whatever they may be. Biases are entrenched rather than challenged which is obviously unhealthy for the proper functioning of a democracy where goodwill and compromise should be encouraged above all.

Any citizen chosen for duty would be, on average, no more or less immune from this chaotic environment than anyone else. The way that the jury system would help in counteracting this atmosphere would be, first, the seriousness of the task, which would be officially and ritually emphasized by way of some sort of swearing in ceremony at the beginning as is now done in a criminal trial and secondly by being embedded among a group of fellow jurors that would, in most cases I believe, encourage a sense of objectivity and high seriousness that is often absent from the usual casual consumption of the media and the sense that they are all participating in an important event. There would be a great emphasis on getting things right as the consequences would often be significant for the functioning of the jurisdiction in question and also that the citizen would, when looking back on this experience, want to take pride in the decisions being made. Although most juries would be dealing with fairly ordinary issues some would be making decisions of historical significance. A jury could also, if they wished, step outside the mainstream media perspective by consulting with outliers regarding the issue under consideration. A citizen can do this anyway, and many often do, but the sense of the importance of their jury duty, of it being a significant event in their lives, would motive most people to consider expanding their perspectives at least for a time, beyond their usual parameters. Being called for jury duty should be considered, as it is in a criminal trial, a kind of sacred duty, crucial to the proper functioning of their society in which they are expected to treat the process seriously and perform in an honorable manner where they would be willing to reconsider any of the normal and everyday opinions they may have formed over their lives and work with the other jurors and consultants to arrive at the best conclusion possible.

The question of media regulation would be a very particular one depending on the jurisdiction involved and would no doubt, under a free and democratic regime, differ substantially between state and private media networks, the state network being much more controllable considering that in most jurisdictions it is considered to have a mission of service to the society as a whole and is understood to be required to officially serve such a mandate. One would expect that the state media would more closely reflect the differing perspectives of the population since it is the population, through jury system regulation, that would have the influence over this institution that is now wielded by politicians and their political parties. Multiple juries over time, being called to review the performance of the state broadcaster, would contain a good demographic and ideological cross section of the society and any legitimate group would no doubt make their voices heard if they felt their interests were being ignored. The state broadcaster would fulfil its mandate much more completely than in our present world where it is often captured by ideological interest groups and political parties.

As I have said, state-run media must keep the politicians happy and under JD the politicians would no longer exist, but private media must keep their advertisers happy which sets up a different dynamic. Private media would have much more leeway in what they report and would often be constrained by little more than avoiding legal penalties for malicious slander but as large media companies draw money from a wide variety of advertisers the pressure to edit information cannot be denied. Particularly large corporations who can afford to advertise on all the major channels can often buy the silence of the media or at least influence the degree of attention given to certain sensitive issues and when they also advertise on state-run media, most whom accept ad money from private businesses, the chances for controlling the narrative grows even stronger. And one must remember that private media enterprises are themselves often very large and very rich and are often owned by huge non-media conglomerates, an example being Amazon CEO Jeff Bezos owning the Washington Post. Most of the so-called independent media are actually owned by much larger conglomerates as well. I will not go into any more detail as I want to keep this book concise but this information can be found by anyone who wished to explore the subject; the point being that much of the "news" that reaches the viewer is much less objective and much more controlled by non-media forces than most people realize. If an individual, and I recommend this as an exercise in media literacy, wishes to dig into a topical media story he will often find that the reportage is quite different than the actual facts that they proport to cover. Some facts get reported and some get left out and the reported facts are often framed in such a way as to insinuate a foregone conclusion of some interested party or parties as there are often multiple interests; corporate sponsors, politicians, the personal ideological biases of journalists and very often the lazy, conformist, herd-like behavior of those same journalists.

To explore a classic example of the hive-mind behavior of mainstream journalism read the book "Columbine" by Dave Cullen on the Columbine High School massacre which took place in 1999 and went on to influence the whole subsequent "anti-bullying" agenda. It brilliantly shows the vast gulf between the media narrative presented to the public and the actual reality of what transpired and the motives of the perpetrators. It took the better part of a decade for Cullen to uncover much of the data as it had been buried by local law enforcement authorities as it revealed their incompetence in dealing with the matter. The shooters Dylan and Klebold were not bullying victims but juvenile delinquents with sealed criminal records due to their age and who had meticulously planned the assault on Columbine High School for two years, fantasizing that the attack would spark a great revolution. Rather than bullied victims they were Nietzscheans who saw themselves in almost god-like terms with the right to destroy their fellow students who they viewed as their inferiors. In other words the truth was vastly different than the narrative presented by the media who behaved like veritable lemmings in the level of conformity in which they presented this tragedy. What could be done about this, other than encouraging more independent journalists like Cullen, is anyone's guess. I merely present the case here as a warning to be very skeptical of mainstream journalism and to always have a big question mark at the forefront of your mind when watching the news.

Modern politicians must also pay close attention to the media in order to get ahead of any controversy that may affect them but this leads too much to a "putting out fires" type of governance since the media is, and always has, operated on a sensationalist "if it bleeds it leads" philosophy along with the adoption of the "clickbait" strategy of so much of the online media. They love to play gotcha journalism. There is a perpetual power struggle between politicians and the media which is baked into the representative style of democracy itself and is not curable under that system and is inherent in a free media that is not mere propaganda.

Under the citizen jurist style of juristical democracy this dynamic would be radically different. The gotcha style of journalism would not work as there would be no-one to "get" at least in the political realm. A jury of randomly chosen citizens would be only temporarily in charge of the process only to be dissolved when the decision is complete when the citizens go back to their regular lives. Gone would be the sometimes too personal love/hate relationship between politicians and journalists that now plague our systems. Those senior bureaucrats that might have a prominent public role which would expose them to media criticism would be vetted and monitored by revolving juries and not politicians and parties and would therefore not be as vulnerable to the "media swarming" style of pressure. They would be evaluated by a jury who could take their time and be more considered than a sensationalist media.

Then there is the politicians fear of running afoul of any number of interest groups who have raised the art of taking offence to a high level and who will target, justifiably or not, both private and public institutions. Indeed it seems for some of these groups finding offence has become a new business model used to extract resources from any institution they can shake down, like a new version of organized crime; "nice business you have here; wouldn't want to see it get broken", and by the way, we would like you to establish this new subsidy, regulation, program, etc., otherwise we will be forced to yell louder. The media love covering a good fight so these groups often receive much more attention than their numbers warrant. Again, this is inherent to an open society, my point being that by removing the politician from the mix and replacing his self-serving decisions with the decisions of a citizen jurors, whose temporary position and power would render them far more immune to the desires of these interest groups. No politicians, no parties, no problem.

The primary source of the ordinary citizen for all things scientific is the media whether this is regarding proper nutrition, environmental issues, the present pandemic, the usual "studies show" kind of reporting. This strategy most people take is to trust that the media has done an acceptable job in vetting the data and is presenting an reasonably accurate view which may or may not be true. It depends on the policy and personal of the particular media outlet and the constituency they serve. In this time of covid hysteria it would be comforting to think that the media would be there to offer a rational and sober vetting process regarding the pandemic, but journalists are people too and are susceptible to group think as much as anyone. Most journalists have zero scientific training so if the information emanating from the expert class is inaccurate it would be difficult and time consuming for them to get up to speed enough to provide any kind of cogent critique. They could consult more experts but the problem with this is that in many fields the experts are required to belong to a central professional organization which could decide to disallow the individual expert to speak freely. This happens much more that people realize which shows that many professional organizations purportedly set up to regulate the standards of the profession for the safety of the public could also be considered to be economic cabals whose less savory purpose is to limit the necessary credentialism required to practice thus limiting the numbers of practitioners so as to keep income high. As I have mentioned elsewhere in this book, how many unemployed doctors and lawyers do you know? Experts are also often dependent on funding from either a corporation or bureaucracy to pursue their studies and so must mind their tongues lest they irritate their paymasters.

Under JD the relevant experts would be interacting much more with the public via the jury system. They could even request anonymity in order to present information that would be otherwise reluctant to talk about for fear of repercussion.

Then there is the fickle attention span of the public itself. Let's face it, we all love observing the new, the weird and the wonderful from the safe distance of our screens and science is as subject to this kind of sensationalism as anything else. Presenting a nuanced, fact-based, often tedious presentation by some boring nerd is for most people far down on the list. A jury would take that nerd far more seriously as the very process in which they are engaging would be far more serious and consequential that our usual random casual viewing.

Consultants

The category of consultant includes the category of the official expert but could be anyone that the jury decides that they would like to speak with. They could not compel anyone to speak or attend as in a criminal trial and the issues of any kind of financial remuneration or transportation costs would be something worked out in an individual basis. The jury may decide it worth their while, under the circumstances, to travel to a certain location instead.

There should not be any pre-set criteria or standards for anyone to present themselves as a consultant to the jury or be requested by the jury to appear before them. There will no doubt be an industry of consulting firms with a roster of experts in various fields who would offer their services to juries; this is to be expected and there is nothing inherently wrong with it. It would only become a problem if certain qualifications were mandated or prohibited by a bureaucracy. Although it would be wise for the preliminary jury to show respect and deference for credentialed individuals who are recognized professionals in their respective fields, the jury can consult with anyone they choose including any critics of the status quo. Outliers and eccentrics would be not be excluded. Juries would also be encouraged to conduct field research if appropriate. If, for example, a factory were to be built in or near a certain neighborhood then the jury would be wise to consult both technical experts and also talk to the inhabitants of the neighborhood as well who would, after all, have to live with the results of their decision. Travel to the proposed construction site would also be encouraged as there is no substitute for a first-hand view.

Classified Military and State Secrets

No military or intelligence agency in any country should ever be allowed to operate unmonitored for obvious reasons. This category would be the one where the most caution and discretion would be required for jury selection. This is the area that would have the highest likelihood for the formation of cabals and for the abuse of power via classified information. One cannot have a high staff turnover as individuals with decades long experience would be preferred. The vetting process undertaken by the preliminary jury would have to be extremely stringent and would have to contain severe penalties for any juror who violates the pact that they would have to enter to be privy to classified information. Individuals chosen would have to be of the highest level of integrity and trustworthiness and possessing of an extraordinary level of knowledge and experience. These juries should be drawn from senior individuals in the business, scientific, diplomatic and academic world with long experience in their respective fields and should be the only juries that would sit for long periods of time as the fewer people who are privy to these secrets the less chance there would be any leaks and also the more time the jurors would have to familiarize themselves with the issues many of which would have extremely complex geo-political and historical intricacies. This would include classified R&D, secret missions, plans for any number of future operations that the military is expected to be ready for and the capacities of intelligence agencies and what kind of tactics they would be permitted to use. Jurors should not have any previous ties, either professional, business or familial with any members of the agency under review although former or retired members of the military or intelligence organization could be consulted by the jury if desired.

Scientific Policy

The setting of long term scientific policy could be set in a number of ways. It would be neither necessary nor desirable to have juries micro-managing policy. The truth of the matter is that scientific progress is largely a slow, messy, incremental process with an occasional breakthrough that gets the publicity. Government scientific institutions can be seen as just another bureaucracy that would be treated like any other; open to periodic review from a viewpoint of efficacy and financial viability. Scientific research is also largely an academic and industrial exercise and would be driven by much of what transpires in the ever-changing conditions in other nations and industries. Governments do have their own research facilities and a healthy scientific ecosystem would allow multiple actors operating in a largely uncoordinated environment in which outcomes, as is almost always the case with science, would be unpredictable. The scientist can however bypass the bureaucracy of his own institution and appeal to a jury to mandate the financing of new research or to review the present work of a government funded program which he believes is no longer bearing fruit or has been in some way corrupted. This stepping outside of the scientific consensus would probably have negative ramifications for the scientists career but if the scientist can persuade a jury of his case and get them to step in and reorganize the institution or even finance the scientist independently then this would be a useful mechanism of discipline and correction that would help prevent the scientific establishment from becoming complacent or corrupt. There would always be the possibility for a rogue scientist, or anyone else for that matter, to use the jury system to shake things up. The jury system would have less influence over university departments and industry unless public money is being provided to those institutions for funding. There is no reason however that a jury could not mandate that an independently funded alternative be explored. This decision, which would usually be expensive, could be merely left as a recommendation at present and handed to another jury to explore the decision from a budgetary point of view. Large expensive decisions may take several phases involving multiple juries before any definitive decision would take place. Thus a jury could, in the process of reviewing the progress of a scientific issue or research entity, decide that a drastic change need take place without specifying the exact nature of the change due to time constraints and the complexity of the issue. It would set the issue on a timeline for review by another jury at a later date giving the parties involved time to organize themselves to present their case to a future jury. So aside from the preliminary, main and final jury triad there could be a series of jury groups forming and dissolving and involving multiple steps until any final decision is made.

Industrial Policy

Although in the United States in free market circles especially it is frowned upon to even think of having an industrial policy and instead "letting the market decide", in the light of recent policies and actions by China this policy looks increasingly negligent and even reckless. The recent Covid-19 pandemic has revealed in a very dramatic fashion our serious vulnerability to frayed and broken supply chains to impact our societies in many serious ways. From pharmaceuticals to rare earth metals necessary for the manufacture of critical components our vulnerability has been starkly revealed. All countries need an industrial policy on many levels and, no, the market cannot decide. The world has been revealed as full of unreliable and even hostile actors, in fact it always was, we just blinded ourselves to this fact in the case of China so as to not be shut out of such a vast market. But even usually trusted allies cannot always be depended upon. During severe shortages, such as the recent PPE shortage during the pandemic, allies kept critical supplies for their own citizens first and understandably so. Critical stockpiles can only be financed and maintained by governments either directly or by mandate. Critical industries producing strategic products must be protected, either by tariff or subsidy, from destruction by foreign competition. It is fine for non-critical industries such as clothing, toys and certain consumer products to be produced by foreigners, even ones of dubious repute such as China but enough of a domestic economy to provide sufficient security during times of war or pandemics without relying on other countries should be prioritized and periodic reviews of these matters should be required. Obviously not all industries can or should be domestically based; the principle of comparative advantage has its place and many foreign countries can be trusted to secure many goods but the security of the aforementioned critical supplies and infrastructure must be prioritized. The jury system would better reflect the general priorities of a nation and would counteract the corporate practice of indiscriminately off-shoring production and creating the vulnerabilities stated above.

The Educational System

I'm not going to get too prescriptive here as there are many ways to educate. The so-called normal school system as is common throughout most of the west is a product of the 19th century factory system and leaves much to be desired. There is no reason in this day and age to limit ourselves to it and as the recent pandemic shows the system can certainly change, and rather quickly if need be. The growing trend to homeschool is also a proven option and might even be considered the primary method as it is only natural for parents to have the ultimate choice over how their children are educated. And let's not get started on the mess that is higher education where students are hoodwinked into what can in many cases only be referred to as a kind of indentured servitude to the financial institutions who are underwriting their loans since they are legally prohibited, at least in the U.S., to declare bankruptcy under any circumstances and so where they leave with enormous debts and a degree that is often worse than useless and will hobble them financially for most of their adult life. If any other business sold such a product they would have been sued out of existence long ago. Hint hint.

What I want to speak to here is the use of the educational system to essentially produce good jurors. By the time someone graduates high school or reaches adulthood and the age of eligibility for jury duty they should have been taught the multiple intellectual and social skills to make them effective jurors. This would include the basics of scientific and statistical analysis; e.g., "what are the different levels of validity that go into deciding whether a scientific study should be taken seriously or not. How to evaluate the qualifications of a witness or consultant; interviewing techniques; cases where it is beneficial for members of a jury to stay together as a team vs splitting up into smaller groups or individuals; how to write up a coherent decision for presentation to the final jury; there are others I'm sure.

But probably the best education for students would be to be able to observe real juries in action over a period of time and in multiple cases by allowing a certain period of time in the later years of their schooling to participate in a kind of apprenticeship or monitoring program where they would actually form a shadow jury and participate in the process but without having a formal vote. This would give them real experience in case they are ever called for jury duty and even if never called they would at least have a better understanding of how the system works. After all, the way things are supposed to work in theory and the way they work in the actual world are often quite far apart. There is no substitute for real world experience and its superiority over theory, as a quick glance at the deranged wankery emanating from our universities will show. The professoriate are intelligent but most of them have never left school and never run anything except their mouths, and it shows.

On the Covid-19 Pandemic

I hesitated to include this section in the book as I am well aware that many sincere people of good-will have basically accepted the official narrative in regard to the covid-19 pandemic response which is understandable if they obtain their news from mainstream sources, which I have learned long ago to distrust, and that I risk alienating a good percentage of my potential readership, but on this subject I cannot remain silent. It also gives me an opportunity to point out how JD would have vastly improved the response to this crisis.

To observe the machinations of our elites during this pandemic has merely multiplied my contempt for them. With a few exceptions I believe them to be the worst ruling class in western history. They are beyond the pale. To watch their behavior during the last two years of the covid-19 response is to observe an unparalleled display of incompetence, venality, contradictory pronouncements, back pedaling, colossal stupidity, sociopathic indifference to suffering, neurotic control-freakery and in many cases what an objective observer can only characterize as a barely concealed sadism. Where did these people come from? How did so many of the seemingly reasonable politicians who had been on the national scene for years and even decades and that we thought that we knew, morph overnight into such authoritarians? The disconcerting answer, the one you do not want to hear, is that this is who they always were. "Power does not corrupt, it reveals" wrote biographer Robert Caro. The reason that they are behaving this way now and not before is because before they did not have the opportunity to do so. They not only have the opportunity now, they have the approval of large swaths of the population. Previously laboring in a profession viewed by the public as a necessary evil they find that they can now torment a populace, psychologically terrorized into submission by a politicized media and scientific establishment, that not only tolerates the whip but loves the whip and begs for more. Oh, joy! It's the S & M relationship they could only previously admit in their dreams. One of the reasons, perhaps the main reason, that many people go into politics in the first place is that they they are the kind of person that loves making up rules and forcing other people to follow them. This is revealed in the frequency that they are caught breaking their own rules. You must understand that these are *their* rules, not yours. They own them. They make them and you follow them; got it!

This has been enormously stressful and confusing to the citizenry and I will not claim that if this process was governed by a citizen jury rather than the usual authorities that everything would be straightforward and simple, but one of the main problems is that the process has become politically polarized along party lines increasing the already serious tensions among the populace. I am not claiming that polarization and compromises would not happen under JD but I believe it would be much less likely and much less contentious. For one thing the usual megalomaniacs, i.e. politicians, would not be involved, merely ordinary citizens in consultation with experts that *they* had chosen rather than career bureaucrats with who-knows-what agendas motivating them. Big Pharma with it's bottomless financial resources would be forced to be transparent, making it much more difficult to manipulate the R&D process and the public health bureaucracy. Shadowy money-men bearing gifts would be considered criminals and treated as such. This does not mean that the juries would always make the right choices but the process would be much more transparent than the present mess which is creating such conflict and resentment. The initial decision to lockdown at the beginning of the pandemic would probably have been made by public health authorities, there would have been no time to form a jury on such quick notice, but any subsequent lockdowns along with any other policies would be continuously monitored by a citizen jury to which the bureaucracy would have to justify every decision. There was no public debate to impose the subsequent lockdowns as there should have been. It was by political decree as have been all the lockdowns and mandates since. Under JD these decisions would have been democratically reviewed from the beginning and continuously thereafter. Once the demographic pattern of infection was clear and a reasonable risk assessment was possible, the whole question of lockdowns, quarantines, masks and vaccines would have been brought under control of the jury system where, in consultation with experts _chosen by the jury,_ the details of these policies would have been worked out rather than by scientifically illiterate politicians following the recommendations of dodgy lifetime bureaucrats or public health officials whose salary and positions depended on these politicians or by the deeply compromised World Health Organization or by doctors and scientists whose research funds are controlled by the CDC and NIH.

About the Author

Peter Hayward is an independent writer who lives in the province of Nova Scotia, Canada.